GREGORY L. VOGT

JUPITER

The Millbrook Press
Brookfield, Connecticut

Published by The Millbrook Press
2 Old New Milford Road
Brookfield, Connecticut 06804

Library of Congress Cataloging-in-Publication Data

Vogt, Gregory.
Jupiter/Gregory L. Vogt.
p.   cm.—(Gateway solar system)
Includes bibliographical references and index.
Summary: Presents information about the
largest planet in our solar system and its moons.
ISBN 1-56294-329-4 (lib. bdg.)
1. Jupiter (Planet)—Juvenile literature.
[1. Jupiter (Planet) 2. Planets.] I. Title.
II. Series: Vogt, Gregory. Gateway solar system.
QB661.V64   1993
523.4'5—dc20   92-30187   CIP   AC

Photographs and illustrations courtesy
National Aeronautics and Space Administration

Solar system diagram by Anne Canevari Green

JUPITER

A *Voyager* picture of Jupiter shows the Great Red Spot, an oval-shaped area at the bottom, center. The spot, a huge storm, is three times wider than Earth.

It is easy to see why Jupiter is called the giant planet. It is larger than all the other planets of the solar system combined. If Mercury, Venus, Earth, Mars, Saturn, Uranus, Neptune, and Pluto were lumps of clay and you could squeeze them all together, they still wouldn't be as big as Jupiter.

Jupiter is hundreds of millions of miles from Earth. But we can see it shining brightly in the night sky. Thus people have studied Jupiter since ancient times. In recent years, spacecraft have helped us learn about the giant planet.

Many wonderful and mysterious things make Jupiter very different from Earth. Before we look at these discoveries, let's review some of the basic things we know about the sun's largest planet.

The Fifth Planet

Jupiter has a diameter of 88,849 miles (142,984 kilometers). That's 11 times bigger than Earth! The pull of Jupiter's *gravitation* is much stronger than Earth's, too. (Gravitation is a force that causes objects to attract each other.) Because Jupiter's gravitational pull is so strong, an object would weigh more on Jupiter than it would on Earth. If you weighed 50 pounds (23 kilograms) on Earth,

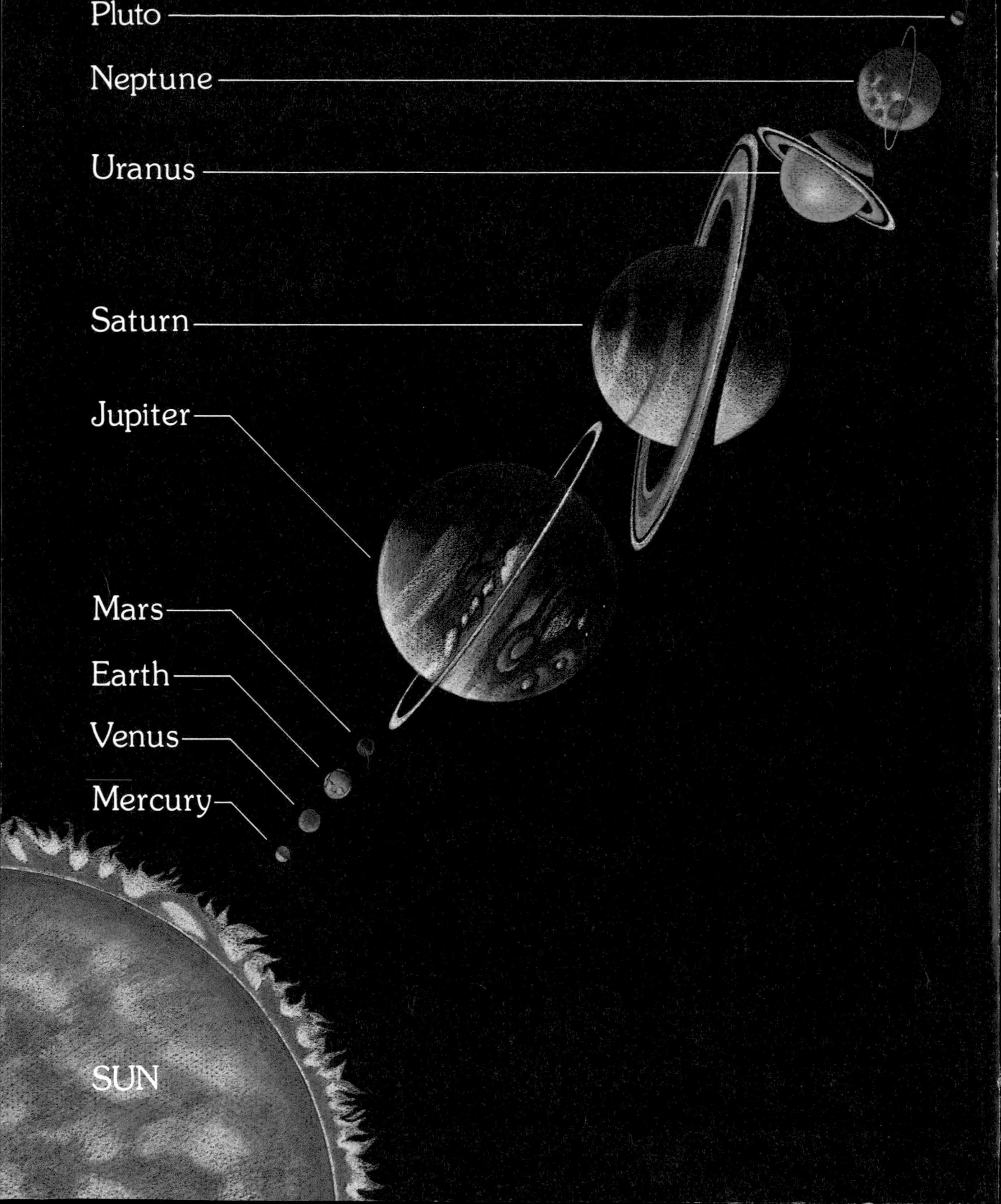

Pluto

Neptune

Uranus

Saturn

Jupiter

Mars

Earth

Venus

Mercury

SUN

you would weigh 127 pounds (58 kilograms) on Jupiter—more than two and a half times as much.

Jupiter is the sun's fifth planet. It is 483 million miles (778 million kilometers) from the sun, five times farther than Earth is. Because it is farther away, Jupiter takes longer to *orbit* (travel around) the sun. A year on Jupiter is 12 Earth years long!

A Jupiter year is long, but a Jupiter day is short. A day on Jupiter is a little less than ten hours long. This is the time the planet takes to spin once on its *axis,* an imaginary line drawn through its center from its north pole to its south pole. Jupiter spins almost two and a half times faster than Earth does.

Because Jupiter is farther from the sun than Earth is, it receives less of the sun's warmth and light. On Earth, the sun shines about twenty-four times brighter than it does on Jupiter.

But if you lived on Jupiter, the sun's brightness might not matter much. You probably would not be able to see the sun anyway. You would see only clouds.

A World of Clouds

Unlike Earth, Jupiter doesn't have a solid surface. Nearly all the planet is made up of gas, and the gas is very cloudy. Jupiter's gases are mainly hydrogen and helium,

Jupiter's atmosphere is filled with light and dark clouds that swirl around the planet in different directions.

with small amounts of other gases like methane, ammonia, and water vapor.

Let's suppose we can take an imaginary trip inside Jupiter. We will see some interesting changes in the gases as we go deeper toward the planet's center.

The cloudy upper layers of the planet are made of very thin gas. Here the temperature is a chilly 200 degrees below zero Fahrenheit (−130 degrees Celsius). Remember, there isn't much heat from the sun to warm the gas. But, as we go deeper, the gas gets heavier and much warmer.

It may not seem like it, but gas has weight. The gas in the upper layers presses down on the gas beneath, squeezing it so that the lower layers of gas become denser, or more compact. Soon, the pressure is so great that the gas turns into a liquid.

Even deeper inside Jupiter, the liquid hydrogen gas turns into a liquid metal. By now, the temperatures inside Jupiter may have climbed to thousands of degrees. Finally, we come to what some *astronomers* (scientists who study objects in space) believe may be a core made of very hot melted rock and water in Jupiter's center.

An astronaut orbiting Earth sees land, water, and swirling white clouds. An astronaut orbiting Jupiter would have a very different view. Instead of swirling white clouds, the astronaut would see parallel bands of brightly colored clouds. The bands stretch completely around the planet like fat latitude lines on a world globe. The bands alternate in color from white to reddish brown and orange.

Astronomers call these bands *belts* and *zones*. The belts are streams of clouds made of sulfur compounds. They are blowing around the planet at high speed in a westerly direction.

The clouds in the zones are made up of white am-

Jupiter's light and dark clouds race around the planet in circular belts and zones. This picture, pieced together from many *Voyager* pictures, shows Jupiter's Southern Hemisphere. The dark shape in the center is a spot where the pictures didn't overlap. This is the location of Jupiter's south pole.

monia ice crystals. They are blowing in the opposite direction, to the east. Looked at from the side, belts and zones are like waves on an ocean. Belts are high, like wave crests, and zones are low, like wave troughs.

The moving belts and zones of Jupiter's upper atmosphere produce beautiful color patterns. When two streams of gas flow in opposite directions, there is friction—the bands rub against each other. Swirls begin to form at the boundary between the streams. You can see this effect for yourself if you fill a bathtub with water. Let the water become very still. Then place your hands at opposite ends of the tub and drag them slowly through the water so that they pass near each other. Your hands will make swirling currents of water.

The swirls on Jupiter are like hurricane storms on Earth. The largest of these swirls is called the *Great Red Spot.* For more than 300 years, astronomers have observed this football-shaped spot in the planet's southern *hemisphere,* near the *equator.* The spot is huge. It is nearly as long as three planet Earths placed side by side.

The Great Red Spot is actually a mammoth storm swirling about in a clockwise direction. Its winds travel at 225 miles (362 kilometers) per hour. In the center of the

Great swirls of colored gas are created where Jupiter's belts and zones rub against each other. This picture has been processed with a computer to make the colors brighter than they really are, to show details.

A close-up of Jupiter's Great Red Spot. The colors have been brightened by computer.

storm, dark-colored gases from within the planet bubble upward. Astronomers think the storm could be a million years old.

Exploring Jupiter

Before astronomers had robot spacecraft to explore the solar system, they had to be content to study planets like Jupiter with their telescopes. Big telescopes could make

Jupiter appear very close, but there was one problem. The light coming to Earth from space had to pass through Earth's atmosphere to reach their telescopes.

The air in Earth's atmosphere is not very clear. It shimmers from heat currents, and it has dust and pollution in it. Air also acts like a filter that blocks out some of the *radiation* (energy given off by warm or hot objects) from space. Because of Earth's atmosphere, even with the biggest telescopes, Jupiter still looked blurred to astronomers. But the view cleared up when the first *interplanetary* robot spacecraft traveled out into our solar system. With television camera systems, these spacecraft

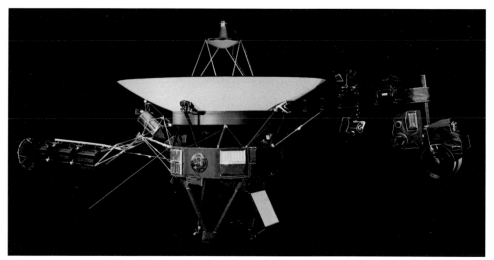

Voyager has a large white dish antenna for radio communications with Earth. On the right side of the spacecraft are television cameras and other scientific instruments for studying Jupiter. On the left are power supplies for running the spacecraft.

were able to take close-up pictures of the planets and radio them back to Earth.

The first of these robot spacecraft explorers to reach Jupiter arrived in the middle 1970s. Two U.S. spacecraft, *Pioneer 10* and *Pioneer 11,* traveled hundreds of millions of miles through space and passed by Jupiter. It took them about two years to get there!

An artist's drawing of how a *Voyager* spacecraft appeared as it approached Jupiter.

A few years later, two more U.S. spacecraft, *Voyager 1* and *Voyager 2*, also made the trip. Recently, a fifth spacecraft, *Ulysses*, also visited Jupiter. This spacecraft made a loop around the giant planet and then headed back toward the sun, where it would fly over the sun's north and south poles.

Each of these spacecraft radioed back data about Jupiter and the moons that circle it. All but *Ulysses* sent back exciting pictures.

Many of the most exciting discoveries made about Jupiter and its moons came from the *Voyager* spacecraft. As *Voyager 1* flew by Jupiter, it pointed its cameras back toward the sun. It saw a faint line running around the planet. The line was a dusty ring that began about 18,000 miles (30,000 kilometers) above the cloud tops and extended up to about 80,000 miles (129,000 kilometers).

Jupiter was the third planet found to have a ring. The other two known to have rings were Saturn and Uranus. Later, rings were also found around Neptune. The rings are formed of particles of rock and ice.

The reason astronomers hadn't known that Jupiter had a ring was that the ring was much too faint to see from Earth. One scientist estimated that the material in the ring was 10,000 times more transparent than glass. The ring became visible to *Voyager 1* only when the

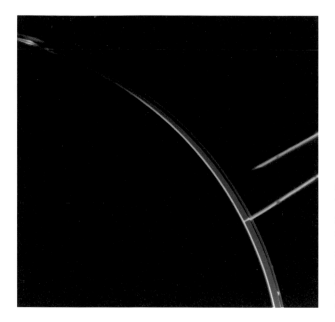

A small segment of Jupiter's ring. Because the spacecraft was moving as the picture was taken, the edge of Jupiter appears as a red, white, and blue line.

spacecraft was on the opposite side of Jupiter from the sun. The sun's light was scattered by the dust and other particles that made up the ring. This is similar to the way dust in the air inside a room scatters the light from sunbeams coming through a window.

Jupiter's Moons

Other great discoveries made by spacecraft include the first close-up views of some of Jupiter's moons. Jupiter has at least 16 moons, or *satellites*. (A satellite is a small body that orbits a larger body in space. Moons are "natural satellites" that orbit planets. Orbiting spacecraft are sometimes called "artificial satellites" because they are made by humans.) Before the *Voyagers* arrived, astronomers knew of only 12 moons.

Four of the moons are very large. They are called the *Galilean satellites* after the Italian astronomer Galileo Galilei, who discovered them with a small telescope nearly 400 years ago. The biggest of the four satellites is called *Ganymede.* It is the largest satellite in the solar system. With a diameter of 3,270 miles (5,262 kilometers), it is larger than the planets Mercury or Pluto!

Ganymede's surface is peppered with *meteor* cra-

An artist's drawing of how the complete ring of Jupiter would appear. The ring is drawn around a photograph of Jupiter.

Jupiter's four Galilean satellites. Io, in the upper left, is the size of Earth's moon. Below Io is Ganymede. Europa is top right, with Callisto beneath.

ters. (Meteors are bits of rock or metal that shoot through space. When they strike a solid moon or a planet, they blast out holes or craters.) The craters make the giant satellite look like Earth's moon. Many of the craters have bright centers, which tell astronomers that the crust of Ganymede is made up of ice that is covered with dust and rock. Each time a meteor strikes the moon, clean ice from below is blasted upward and makes a light spot in the dark surface. Many Ganymede craters even have light-colored rays extending outward across the surface, like the spokes of bicycle wheels.

In other areas of Ganymede's surface, there are

This closer view of Ganymede reveals many craters and bright lines across the surface. The blue and orange dots were added by *Voyager*'s cameras and are not part of Ganymede.

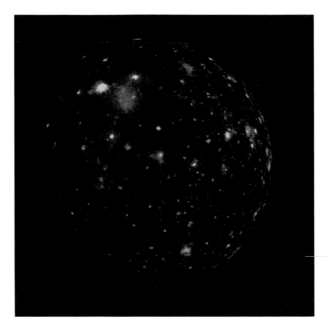

The surface of Callisto, Jupiter's second-largest moon, is peppered with meteor craters.

parallel lines snaking about. The surface looks as if someone had dragged a giant rake across it. Astronomers think that Ganymede's surface has been pushed and wrinkled by large movements similar to earthquakes on Earth.

The second of Jupiter's big moons is *Callisto.* It is only a few hundred miles smaller in diameter than Ganymede. Astronomers think the moon might have large amounts of water inside it. Callisto's surface is very old. Except for meteor impacts, the surface is fairly smooth. Callisto has no hills or mountains. When you look at the moon's surface, meteor craters are the features that stand out. This moon has more craters than any other known

Jupiter's Io looks like a giant cheese pizza.

moon in the solar system—so many that it is like the solar system's shooting gallery. Some of the meteorites hit Callisto's surface so hard that huge craters were left behind and are surrounded by many circular cracks.

The third largest of the big moons is *Io* (pronounced eye-oh). Io offered great surprises for the astronomers who were a part of the *Voyager* teams. In pictures, this moon looked like a huge cheese pizza, 2,256 miles (3,630 kilometers) across! Io's surface is brightly colored in yellow, orange, white, brown, and black. The colors show that the moon's surface is rich in sulfur compounds.

The biggest Io discovery came when astronomers

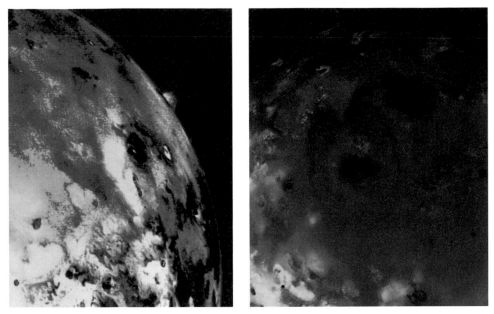

Left: One of Io's sulfur volcanoes erupting. The bluish cloud of sulfur, blown upward in the eruption, rises 100 miles (160 km) above the surface. Right: A close-up of one of Io's volcanoes shows a dark, heart-shaped outline where debris thrown out by the volcano has settled back on the surface.

studied the horizons of the moon. Faint dome-shaped clouds were visible in a few places. Some were nearly 190 miles (306 kilometers) high. The clouds were being created by the eruption of volcanoes! At the time of the discovery, Earth was the only body in the solar system known to have active volcanoes.

Eventually, nine active volcanoes were discovered on Io. The volcanoes were sending out sulfur, oxygen, and sodium at speeds of a half mile (0.8 kilometer) per second. The particles and gases not only rained down on Io. They also spread out around Jupiter in a great, but very thin, cloud stretching millions of miles away from the planet.

Scientists think that Io has volcanoes because it is in the middle of a tug-of-war with Ganymede and *Europa,* the fourth of the big satellites. As these moons orbit Jupiter, they move closer to Io and then farther away. When one of those moons gets near Io, the pull of gravitation between Io and that moon is very strong. The pull of gravitation between the two moons gets weaker when they move apart. The changes in the gravitational pull cause friction within Io. The friction generates heat, and the heat causes the eruptions.

Europa, the fourth Galilean satellite, is about the size of Earth's moon. Europa offered its own surprises. Europa's surface is the smoothest of any moon in the solar system. In fact, Europa looks like a giant billiard ball with cracks.

Scientists believe that Europa has a crust of frozen water ice 18 miles (30 kilometers) thick. The ice is floating on an ocean 50 miles (80 kilometers) deep. Beneath Europa's ocean is a rocky core.

The cracks in Europa are smooth enough to have been painted on with a felt marker. They are believed to result from the same tug-of-war that produces Io's volcanoes.

A close-up of Europa shows details of the moon's many surface cracks.

The rest of Jupiter's moons are small and rocky or icy. Four of them were discovered by the *Voyager* spacecraft. The closest moon to Jupiter is tiny Metis. Metis is only 25 miles (about 40 kilometers) in diameter. Even smaller is Sinope, just 22 miles (35 kilometers) across. Sinope is the most distant of Jupiter's known moons. It orbits nearly 15 million miles (nearly 24 million kilometers) away.

New Mysteries

One of the remarkable things about the space age is the ability of spacecraft to travel to the planets and gather information and pictures at close range. From the data and pictures collected of Jupiter and its moons, astronomers have been able to make many discoveries. Unfortunately, the close visits of the two *Pioneer,* two *Voyager,* and one *Ulysses* spacecraft each lasted only a few days. Much more could have been learned if the spacecraft had been able to go into orbit around Jupiter.

That is just what scientists hope will happen in 1995 with the NASA *Galileo* spacecraft. For about two years, *Galileo* will orbit Jupiter and fly close to its big moons. *Galileo* will also drop a small probe into Jupiter's atmosphere to study the planet's cloud layers. If all goes well, *Galileo* will make new discoveries and uncover new mysteries of the giant planet.

An artist's drawing shows NASA's *Galileo* leaving the space shuttle for Jupiter.

Jupiter: Named after the Roman god of the heavens and of weather.

	Jupiter	*Earth*
Average Distance From the Sun		
Millions of miles	483	93
Millions of kilometers	778	150
Revolution (one orbit around the Sun)	11.86 years	1 year
Average Orbital Speed		
Miles per second	8	18.6
Kilometers per second	13	30
Rotation (spinning once)	9 hours, 55 minutes	24 hours
Diameter at Equator		
Miles	88,849	7,926
Kilometers	142,984	12,756
Surface Gravity (compared to Earth's)	2.54	1
Mass (the amount of matter contained in Jupiter, compared to Earth)	318	1
Atmosphere	hydrogen helium	nitrogen oxygen
Satellites (moons)	16	1
Rings	1	0

Jupiter's Moons	*Diameter*	*Distance From Planet*
Metis	25 mi	79,513 mi
	40 km	127,960 km
Adrastea*	12 mi	80,147 mi
	20 km	128,980 km

Jupiter's Moons	Diameter	Distance From Planet
Amalthea*	117 mi 188 km	112,658 mi 181,300 km
Thebe*	62 mi 100 km	137,886 mi 221,900 km
Io	2,256 mi 3,630 km	261,977 mi 421,600 km
Europa	1,950 mi 3,138 km	416,889 mi 670,900 km
Ganymede	3,270 mi 5,262 km	664,885 mi 1,070,000 km
Callisto	2,983 mi 4,800 km	1,170,074 mi 1,883,000 km
Leda	10 mi 16 km	6,893,680 mi 11,094,000 km
Himalia	116 mi 186 km	7,133,536 mi 11,480,000 km
Lysithea	22 mi 36 km	7,282,669 mi 11,720,000 km
Elara	47 mi 76 km	7,293,233 mi 11,737,000 km
Ananke	19 mi 30 km	13,173,429 mi 21,200,000 km
Carme	25 mi 40 km	14,043,373 mi 22,600,000 km
Pasiphae	31 mi 50 km	14,602,622 mi 23,500,000 km
Sinope	22 mi 35 km	14,726,899 mi 23,700,000 km

*These moons are not round. The longest dimension is given.

GLOSSARY

Astronomer	A scientist who studies planets, moons, stars, and other objects in outer space.
Axis	An imaginary line running through a planet from its north to its south pole.
Belt	Westward-moving dark clouds circling Jupiter in a band.
Callisto	One of Jupiter's Galilean satellites.
Equator	An imaginary line running around the middle of a planet and halfway between the planet's north and south poles.
Europa	One of Jupiter's Galilean satellites.
Galilean satellites	The four moons of Jupiter that were discovered by Galileo.
Ganymede	One of Jupiter's Galilean satellites.
Gravitation	A force that causes objects to attract each other.
Great Red Spot	A huge hurricane-like storm in Jupiter's southern hemisphere.
Hemisphere	Half of a sphere.
Interplanetary	Between the planets.
Io	One of Jupiter's Galilean satellites.
Mass	The amount of matter contained in an object.
Meteor	A piece of space rock or metal that shoots through space and causes craters when it crashes into solid moons and planets.
Orbit	The path a planet takes to travel around the sun, or a moon to travel around a planet.

Pioneer 10 and *11*	Spacecraft that visited Jupiter in the mid-1970s.
Radiation	Energy given off by warm or hot objects (including radio waves, microwaves, infrared light, visible light, ultraviolet light, X rays, gamma rays).
Revolution	One complete orbit of a planet around the sun, or a moon around a planet.
Rotation	The spinning of a planet or moon around its axis.
Satellite	A small body in space that orbits a larger body. A satellite may be "natural," as a moon, or "artificial," as a spacecraft.
Ulysses	Spacecraft that visited Jupiter in 1991 on its way to the sun's poles.
Voyager 1 and *2*	Spacecraft that visited Jupiter in the late 1970s.
Zone	Eastward-moving light clouds circling Jupiter in a band.

FOR FURTHER READING

Asimov, I. *Jupiter: The Spotted Giant*. Milwaukee: Gareth Stevens, 1989.

Gallant, R. *The Planets, Exploring the Solar System*. New York: Four Winds Press, 1982.

Landau, E. *Jupiter*. New York: Franklin Watts, 1991.

Simon, S. *Jupiter*. New York: William Morrow, 1985.

Vogt, G. *Voyager*. Brookfield, Conn.: The Millbrook Press, 1991.

INDEX

ABOUT THE AUTHOR

Gregory L. Vogt works for NASA's Educational Division at the Johnson Space Center in Houston, Texas. He works with astronauts in developing educational videos for schools.

Mr. Vogt previously served as executive director of the Discovery World Museum of Science, Economics and Technology in Milwaukee, Wisconsin, and as an eighth-grade science teacher. He holds bachelor's and master's degrees in science from the University of Wisconsin at Milwaukee, as well as a doctorate in curriculum and instruction from Oklahoma State University.